Taming The Dragons

Beth Fiedler

DEDICATION

This book is dedicated to my parents, my siblings Eva, Teresa and Leung, my husband Nelson and my best friend Terry, whose support and love continue to inspire me to live the fullest and share what I have learned.

ACKNOWLEDGMENTS

I thank my husband, Nelson, who accompanied me on the *Dragons' Den* journey. I thank him for his continued encouragement and support especially when I occasionally lost confidence in myself.

I thank my elder sister Eva and my best friend Terry who are always there for me whenever I need a pair of patient ears.

I thank my friend, Wilma, who told me about *Dragons' Den*. Her faith in me had motivated us to participate in the first audition.

I thank our producer Scott who has been there for us since our first audition. His guidance and dedication have made substantial differences on our on-stage performance.

I thank Tracie who offered to take our "My Roller Coaster Ride" poster to the Dragons for signatures. It has become an invaluable memoir on our second chance experience.

I thank my Toastmasters peer, Andy, who provided me with constructive feedback and suggestion to enhance our first pitch performance.

I thank my mentor, Elena, whose diligence and professionalism have inspired me to stay focused and persistent in pursuing my dreams.

I thank our family lawyer, Glenn, who has always been there for us.

I thank Bigstock and the image contributor julos for the images used on the inserts.

I am grateful for the opportunity to share my learnings with you.

CONTENTS

INTRODUCTION

The Fiedler's had the first flavor of the *Dragons' Den* experience in March 2013. Our pitch was aired on 22 January 2014 (almost a year after presenting our investment idea to the Dragons).

What motivated us to return for an audition in February 2014? As second chance pitchers, did we stand a better chance to get a deal?

How did we compare our two pitch experiences? With two new Dragons joining Season IX, how did we apply our former Den experience to our second chance?

Having gone through two once-in-a-lifetime experiences, how would we pitch our idea differently and what tips can we share with the entrepreneurs who are anxious to give it a try?

It's my intention to cover our experiences in detail though I must emphasize that they may not cover everything our readers would like to know. I prepared a sign-up page for those who would like to better understand our journey.

This book will serve as a guide to those who are going for an audition. It will help to give them a heads up about what to expect, especially when they receive an invitation to pitch in front of the Dragons. This book will be a useful guide to help them to stay calm throughout the whole experience and feel as though they have accomplished something, regardless of the outcome.

Our Den experiences were overwhelming yet they helped us create a closer bond before, during and post-production. Our heartfelt thanks to the producers and team members of CBC Dragons' Den and the Dragons for these amazing life experiences!

Fast Facts On The CBC Dragons' Den
Source: BBM Canada PPM. Total Canada
9/10/2012-12/9/2012

- #1 Unscripted Canadian entertainment program
- Reaches 1 in 4 Canadians
-10 out of 13 episodes that aired in the Fall 2012 garnered 1 million+ (Ad2+)
- A record 87 handshake deals with more than $13 million invested
- Multi-award winning program: Gemini awards, Canadian Screen Award, Media Innovation Awards, Best reality program at the 2012 Banff World Television Festival
- cbc.ca/dragonsden = 500,000 unique visitors + average time spent on th3e site = 13 minutes + Users likely to be Ad25-54 & HHI $75+

Dragons

Nelson

Kevin

CBC

David

Bruce

The

Jim

VIII

Season

Arlene

Fiedler's

Beth

Den

Auditions

AUDITIONS

What Led To The Auditions

The Fiedler's did not own a television set for years. We had no idea about the *Dragons' Den* TV show and/or the Dragons until one December afternoon in 2012. It all started with a casual chat with Wilma.

I learned that *Dragons' Den* is a Canadian television reality show that debuted in 2006 on CBC Television. Canadian entrepreneurs pitch their business and investment ideas to a panel of five rich entrepreneurial businesspeople (termed "Dragons") in the hope of securing business financing and partnerships.

Each pitch begins with the entrepreneurs naming a specific amount of money they wish to get in exchange of a percentage of their business. The rules stipulate that if the entrepreneurs do not raise at least this amount from the Dragons, they get nothing.

There will be a Question & Answer session immediately after the pitch where the Dragons get more information about the business idea should the pitch be at a conceptual stage or a full-fledged long-term business.

Each Dragon will either make an offer to invest, or will declare that they are "out", meaning they are not interested in the business. Once all five Dragons are "out", the pitch ends.

Intrigued by what Wilma shared with me, I did lots of research on the show. When the auditions schedule was released in early January, I was still undecided if I should go for an audition.

After overcoming the initial reluctance, I visited the CBC portal and submitted an online application on EZ Color Trading Academy on 12 January 2013. Days later I submitted a second application on My Roller Coaster Ride on 16 January. Not many were aware that we actually did two auditions when we attended the auditions on 7 February 2013 at McMaster University.

First Things First

Let me quickly go through what an online application entails.

Part 1   Personal Application
           This section is self-explanatory

Part 2   Business Proposal Basics
           This section is self-explanatory. I knew my business idea inclusive of its stage and investment information available. I also had to fill in an estimated investment amount (our Ask) and knew I could change it at a later date. Our Ask on the application, audition and pitch were all different.

Part 3   Business Proposal Details
           This section took me some time to gather my thoughts. I had to consider:

- Information on my proposed EZ Color Trading Academy
- My operation model and how it could bring in revenue
- My current sales and revenue projection
- What inspired this idea and why I wanted to start this business
- Why I am the best person to run the EZ Color Trading Academy
- Highlights on the sacrifices I made
- Elaborate why I wanted the Dragons to partner with us and how we were going to invest their money

It took me at least three rounds (luckily the system had a save draft feature) to complete Part 3. Then I went through the Agree to Terms & Conditions pages (about six pages) before signing it off and clicked Submit.

The online application portal gave me options to attach photos and video. I included our system logo and photo of the Futures trading system I designed.

Did I think they were critical and played an important role for the selection process? I didn't and still don't think they are. Based on our auditions experiences, I estimate that on-stage performance is the most important to sell your idea to the producers who are doing the screening.

Would I recommend submitting an online application before the audition? Yes, I did.

Why? For the entrepreneurs who did not submit an online application before the audition or who did not bring a copy of their online application to the audition venue, they were asked to complete an application on the spot. For us, it was a time saver that we brought along copies of our online applications for our auditions.

When the auditions schedule was released in early January 2013, we picked the McMaster University location because it was close to home.

We had about three weeks to prepare for our auditions on 7 February 2013. You can imagine how we kept changing our minds (go for it or forget about it) in-between until we had a heart-to-heart talk to lay out the pros and cons. Once we agreed that it was worth trying, we spent our energy and time on preparing for the auditions.

Prep for Auditions

First and foremost "if you ask me" for a proposal to stick will always be the introduction. We only had the first 10 seconds (often shorter) to catch the producers' attention. I also learned from my research that most entrepreneurs would only have about five minutes to present their business idea.

Our two business proposals were investment related. Fear and greed have been the popular emotional challenges for most Futures investors. I started creating photo cards on the five Dragons with different emotional attributes.

I downloaded the Dragons' photos from the CBC Dragons' Den website and added different animated graphics (representing emotions related to fear and greed). To make our proposals appealing to the producers, I created revenue projection charts with quantitative data.

Budget Control

Did we spend a lot of money on the auditions? Not really. Our props were created with materials from a Dollar Store (less than $20). Did we dress up for the auditions? Not at all.

Guess what was the biggest expense item for the auditions? Parking at McMaster University. Since we had no idea about the waiting time (we got the 5th and 6th positions), we decided to go with the whole day parking option.

Rehearsal Made Perfect

I hope you will agree with me that on-stage performance is extremely important for our success. Our audition objective was to be shortlisted so that we would be invited to pitch in front of the Dragons. We spent most of our free time practicing our presentation.

We did not know whether there was a quota on each auditions location, or the producers had team meetings to discuss all pitches to nail down the finalists for the studio production. Based on what we learned, it was the latter, ie they had team meetings going through the pitches.

To stand out from the crowd, we used the following metaphors for our two proposals:

EZ Color Trading Academy (Our Ask: $30,000 in exchange for 15% of our business)

- An impactful opening to impress (EZ Color Trading – Your Gateway to the Futures World! Dual-Dialogue when we said EZ Color Academy – Your Answer to Successful Trading!)

- Use of visual aids (eg colorful photo cards and revenue projection chart in a picture frame)

- Use of animated and interactive gadgets to add more fun and entertainment elements (eg, a magic gravity ball to illustrate the investment market move and shiny squishy bears as the guiding lights to inexperienced Futures learners)

My Roller Coaster Ride (No specific Ask – a mutually agreed royalty term with the Dragon(s))

Our second proposal was a book to be written. It was based on my two years struggle in the Futures world. Since it was an idea and I had not even started writing the book, I must think of something else to make an impact right at the beginning.

What did I do? I sang the following lyrics from the Somewhere Over The Rainbow song:

"Somewhere over the rainbow
Skies are blue
All the dreams that you dare to dream
Really do come true"

Up to this moment, I still believe my singing was the reason we got our first invitation to pitch in front of the five Dragons.

Additional Tips

We did not use any notes except the above listed props to add more dynamic elements to our proposals. There was a Question & Answer session in which we had qualitative and quantitative data in our mind supporting why our proposals were profitable investment options for the producers who represented the five Dragons.

Glimpses Of Our Audition Props

1. EZ Color Trading Academy (A gravity magic ball and Futures trading system that Beth designed)

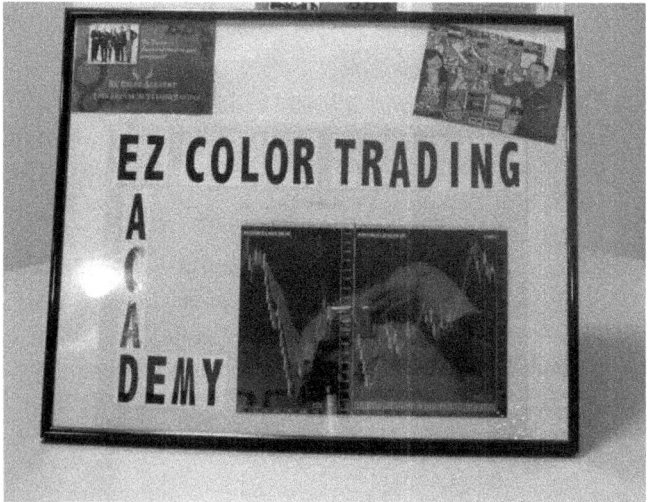

1. EZ Color Trading Academy ((A portable flip-chart with quantitative revenue projection)

1. EZ Color Trading Academy (4"x6" photo cards to give out to the producers)

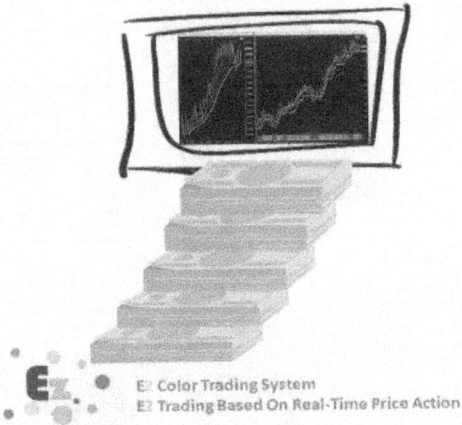

EZ Color Trading System
EZ Trading Based On Real-Time Price Action

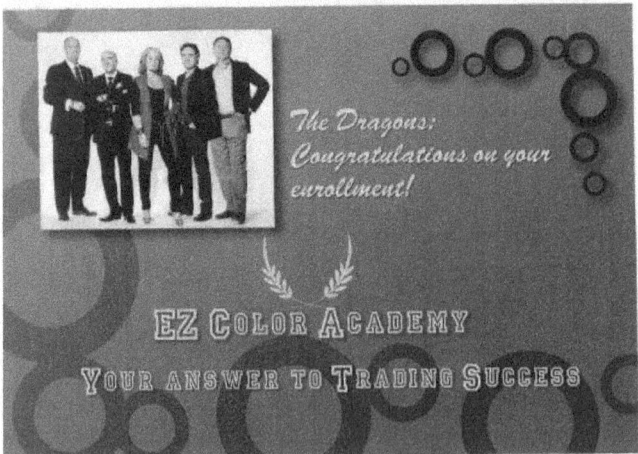

The Dragons:
Congratulations on your
enrollment!

EZ COLOR ACADEMY
YOUR ANSWER TO TRADING SUCCESS

2. My Roller Coaster Ride (4"x6" photo cards - article on Beth's Futures story and shiny squishy bears to add more visual and entertainment elements to our presentation)

EZ Color Training Room

2. My Roller Coaster Ride (A Ride book prototype to hit the point as the book was to be written/published)

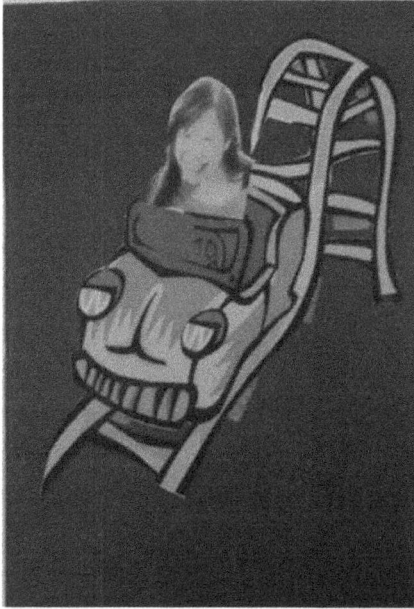

Post-Audition Photo to capture our first experience

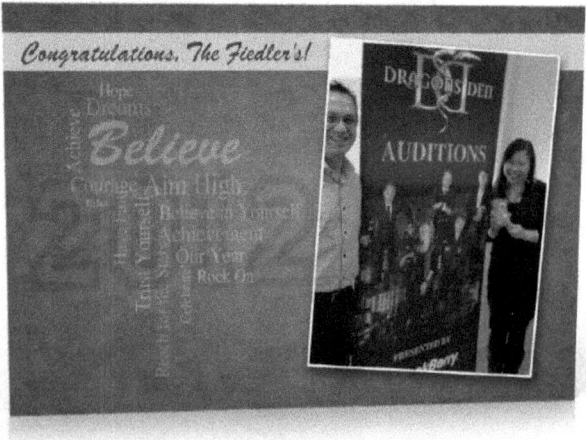

Tick Tock

On the auditions day, we reached the venue around 8:00 am. The audition time schedule was 11:00 am to 6:00 pm. There were four entrepreneurs before us. We waited patiently in the main lobby area until the production team showed up around 10:00 am.

We signed another disclosure agreement while waiting to be called to the audition room. There were about four associates in addition to two associate producers (Katie and Scott) who were the ones listening to all proposals.

Once it was getting closer to our number (5th and 6th), we were called and asked to wait outside the audition room. When the 4th entrepreneur finished his pitch around 1:30 pm, we were given a few minutes to prepare the stage for our first proposal.

We gave our best shot to impress the two producers that we were the real deal. We answered their raised questions to the best of our knowledge. Bear in mind that we had been rehearsing the same proposals for weeks. We watched at least 50 pitches online to familiarize ourselves with the production flow.

Time passed by quickly and the producers thanked us for attending the auditions. Shortlisted entrepreneurs would get an invitation in 3 to 6 weeks.

Post-Auditions

For the first two weeks, we were mesmerized by our auditions experience. We did not tell our family and friends that we went to the auditions. We started to prepare ourselves for not getting an invitation since our proposals were not about physical products that existed.

Based on our research, most of the proposals were product related. When Nelson received a phone call on 26 February confirming that an invitation was on its way. I was in total shock. We got an email the same day with a *Dragons' Den* 2013 Pitcher Guide and a Season VIII Consent & Release agreement. We were also told that an associate producer would be assigned to coach us. As for the exact production date, we would only know in a week or two.

While waiting for the unknown to unfold, I studied the Pitcher Guide diligently and started working on props such as T-shirt and banner design.

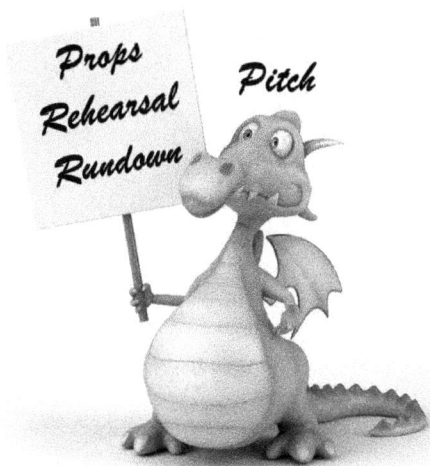

Props Rehearsal Rundown

Pitch

PITCH

What We Learned From The Dragons' Den 2013 Pitcher Guide
  I went through the guide many times to better understand the process of presenting to the Dragons. It covered the following:

1. Logistics

- Location of the CBC production studio (Ours was the CBC's Canadian Broadcasting Centre at John Street, Toronto)

- Tips on Transportation, Accommodations, Travel Arrangement, Arrival Time and Prop Drop-Off

- Rundown from Start to Finish (Our exact experiences would be covered in details under the Behind The Scenes section)

- Additional Guest (We were permitted to bring one family member or friend to accompany us during our taping day unless otherwise approved by our producer. We did not bring any)

2. Presentation Guidelines

This section gave us useful tips on how to make our presentation great. For example, we learned that:

- It was important to make our pitch stand out. Bear in mind that hundreds of entrepreneurs for each Season (about 250) and only the ones with the highest possible entertainment value would be aired.

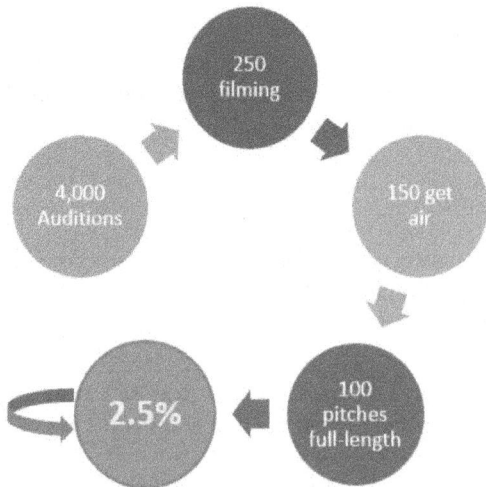

- Dress code. Be creative and avoid all-white clothing or very small patterns and no visible logos of companies or brands.
- Make-Up. Expect basic touch-ups and hair styling. Nothing fancy.

- Posters. Need producer's approval before printing. Must be printed with a matte finish and no lamination. We followed the guide to have our posters mounted on a black foam-core (took us an extra effort to locate a vendor who offered black foam-core). We noticed some entrepreneurs brought along posters mounted on a white foam-core. To play safe, I would recommend complying with the guide.

All posters must be readable from at least five meters away.

- Props. We learned from the guide that it was their preference for us to carry all or most of our presentation materials down the stairs into the Den.

- Documents. Not recommended or allowed before, during or after our presentation. Information inclusive of financial information and profit margins must be conveyed verbally whenever possible.

- Use of Multimedia. Not recommended though could be accommodated with a widescreen television available in the studio. No wireless Internet available inside the studio. Upon endorsement, Internet access could be arranged for our presentation and would be accessed through a studio laptop connected to the television screen.

- Products or handouts to be distributed to the Dragons need the producer's approval. Once they are cleared by the producer, always start out on the right ride of the Dragons when giving out anything to them.

- No more than one or two Dragons are allowed to leave their chairs at one time. Again, the entrepreneurs need prior approval from the producer.

- Designated presentation spot. All presenters must remain standing during the pitch.

Anatomy Of A Pitch

10 essential elements with specific elaboration under the guide. For example,

1) Introduction on the entrepreneurs (Name, hometown, business idea, and Ask in exchange of percentage of equity)

2) Elevator Pitch (Approximately 60 seconds to explain to the Dragons our business proposal inclusive of the product or service in question, its target customers and how can it make money)

3) Demo (An interactive activity or sampling before, after or during our elevator pitch to illustrate what our product or service is and its work mechanism)

Note: The guide alerted us that the Demo could be the most challenging part. It was extremely important to complete our demo before the Dragons' asking too many questions about the business proposal.

4) Q&A (An unstructured discussion with the Dragons that could be anything and everything)

5) Opting "Out" (Walk away after all five Dragons have declared themselves "Out")

6) Investments and 7) Multi-Dragon Investments (Efforts spent to secure a deal matching the Ask amount with one or multiple dragons)

8) Refusing Investment (Entrepreneurs also have the option to refuse a deal)

9) Your Advisor (An option to have an advisor on standby in the "Advisor Room" or place a call to an advisor by telephone (using the telephone located in the "Advisor Room" and will be recorded for possible broadcast)

10) Deal (The "handshake" deal made on the show is an unwritten, non-binding agreement. There would be due diligence checks outside the Den. If a final agreement cannot be reached after the show, no one is legally obliged to complete the deal)

3. How to Prepare Your Pitch

- Guidance on including information to substantiate us as a reliable partner, a profitable business idea with a high return on investment
- Realistic business valuation on our Ask (We learned from the entrepreneurs who participated in the first two seasons. The Dragons reacted strongly to those who over-estimating their valuation)

    Remark: Entrepreneurs can inform their friends, family, community and media about their participation in the show taping, and an airdate. However, they cannot reveal the outcome to anyone until either the segment has been broadcast in an episode or the entire season has completed its original airing.
    We were fortunate to have Scott as our producer who not only endorsed our ideas and prop design promptly, he was there for us to make our presentation more impactful and stand a better chance to be aired.

Preparation Of Season VIII Pitch

Season VIII Dragons:

Arlene Dickinson
Bruce Croxon
David Chilton
Jim Treliving
Kevin O'Leary

Between 26 February and 8 March 2013, while waiting for our producer to contact us, I was working mostly on the pitch and props (poster/T-shirt design and dress code etc). I was uncertain if we should combine our two business ideas (EZ Color Trading (similar to an education center on investment) and to-be written My Roller Coaster Ride book) into one business proposal.

It was great that the waiting time gave me a chance to clear my head. Before our producer Scott reached out to us, we decided to stay with one idea, ie EZ Color Trading Academy.

I had been in close contact with Scott on our pitch. We were extremely grateful for his guidance on the introduction (what elements would make our opening special and entertaining) and Q&A session (when the five dragons would be throwing out questions that we were uninformed as to the nature of).

Challenges On The Way

I estimated that having the Dragons wear a T-shirt with our EZ Color logo would add media exposure to our idea. I placed an order for 10 XXL size before our first call with the producer. Unfortunately, the first design was not approved. The second design was approved for Nelson to wear only. We were not allowed to give them out to the Dragons. We accepted their decision and moved on.

Our second challenge was the song I was originally planning to sing (Somewhere Over the Rainbow). Unless we had clearance, Scott has recommended me to use songs and music with no patent and copyright. For example, Twinkle Twinkle Little Star.

I was reluctant to change my introduction and spent some days finding a way to stay with the original idea. After talking with our family lawyer and some legal friends, I decided to go with Scott's idea and started writing my lyrics using the Twinkle Twinkle Little Star music. You could imagine our excitement when I composed the first version:

EZ EZ Little Star
How you wonder what we are
EZ Trading for Futures
EZ Academy for learning
EZ shows your little light
EZ EZ through the day
EZ EZ Little Star
How you wonder what we are

Of course the final and on-stage version was better:

EZ EZ Little Star
How you wonder what we are
EZ Trading for Futures
EZ Academy for learning
EZ EZ your guiding light
EZ EZ through the day
EZ EZ EZ

Other challenges included most printing companies did not offer black foam-core board for our posters (most onlt offer white foam-core boards). A few did and asked for hundreds of dollars. Luckily, we found an artist store that could do our two posters for around $100.

What was I going to wear? I was very stubborn that I would like to stay with a gypsy outfit. I spent hours online to locate feasible and reasonable options. Upon receipt of the dress, my first shock was that the size was not what I had ordered. It was one size smaller. Time was running out and I was on a diet hoping I could squeeze in on the production date (which I did).

Remember I said the first minute was critical! Having an introduction song was not enough to score high on being dynamic and entertaining. A magic trick idea came to my mind. I was grateful that lots of simple magic tricks were on YouTube. I found one that was easy for Nelson to learn within hours. You would enjoy his rehearsal performance after sign-up for video/photo access.

Guess what were the two most challenging roadblocks?

First, Nelson! He "almost" wanted to quit days before the taping. He worried that he might forget his lines. Or his magic trick would go wrong in front of the Dragons or the production crew could see his flaws when their camera did a close-up to his hands.

We sat down and agreed that getting a deal was unknown. Yet our on-stage performance (except the Q&A session) was within our control. I did my very best to confirm his performance was great. If anything happened on-stage, we could easily laugh it off as if it was part of our presentation.

Our second/last challenging roadblock was our Ask. We made our final change on the taping date and used 50%. Our objective was to perform to the best of our knowledge and capacity so that we would stand a better chance to be aired.

The benefits of being aired was self-explanatory. With or without a Dragon to be our partner, there might be other investors or partners who would get in touch with us for a partnership opportunity.

Did I myself have doubts for the whole Den journey? Yes. There were moments of doubt. Since time and resources were already spent on this *Dragons' Den* pursuit and quitting was never an option, I was grateful that Nelson stood by me and we went through it together.

One Two Three – You Are On

I have covered how we spent our time when we arrived at the CBC studio under the Behind The Scenes section. There were slight differences in the logistics for the first and second Den experiences.

Now let's get to when we were escorted by our producer Scott to an "on deck" lounge for the following:

- Last-minute hair and makeup touch-ups with the help of their stylists
- Assembly of a wireless microphone to our outfit
- A quick microphone level check

Pitch Time

A production team member brought us to the top of the stairs and asked us to wait for the countdown before descending into the Den.

Nelson carried the two posters. Right before taking the stairs down to the Den, we paused and said "hello" and waved to the Dragons from the windows. They waved back to us.

We got to the presentation spots (where the two Xs were) and asked the Dragons to give us a few minutes to set up our posters. Nelson set up the posters on the easel (with the back exposing to the Dragons). I moved two steps closer to the Dragons and sang our introduction lyrics.

It was totally unexpected that most of the Dragons (except Jim) started laughing. Arlene could not hold off laughing while Kevin, Bruce and David made extra efforts to control their emotion.

We overcame the initial shock and continued with our presentation materials. Our Ask: $50,000 in exchange for 50% equity of our business.

Nelson invited Kevin to come to our presentation area and help with his magic trick. His magic trick went well as he succeeded in turning a $20 note into a $100 note.

The Dragons tried to interrupt our presentation several times. For example,

Arlene and Bruce were interested in learning about the following:

How did you both meet?
How long are you married?
Are you happily married?
Did you make money from trading?

We did our best to address their raised questions and went back to our presentation. There were numerous occasions that we had to remind the Dragons politely that we would like to continue with our presentation before getting back to their raised issues. The Dragons accepted our suggestions most of the time.

It was extremely important to finish the crucial part of our presentation before the Q&A session. Once the Dragons began asking many questions about the business and/or other non-related questions (it happened), it would be very difficult to go back.

As of this moment, I still believe that we managed the stage well. It was unfortunate that most the Dragons knew nothing about Futures (where our premise was). They were not in a position to partner with us on the EZ Color Trading Academy idea.

Our pitch lasted for about 15 minutes. The Dragons had requested me to sing the introduction song again. They apologized that Arlene's laughter had distracted them. They promised to pay attention to the lyrics the second time.

I sang my masterpiece a second time with the hope that they appreciated the efforts spent in preparing our presentation. Jim was the first Dragon who was "out". Bruce and David followed suit. Arlene knew nothing and was out as well. Kevin was the last Dragon who stayed at the end before declaring himself "out".

All Dragons treated us professionally. No names were called throughout the whole presentation. We understood that we were treading strange waters where they were not comfortable in investing their money.

We wished them Happy Easter and left the Den gracefully. Right outside the Den, our producer Scott and a camera crew member were waiting for us. Scott asked us to share our personal opinions of the Dragons and our plan for our business.

Nelson responded to the camera saying "We will be back". We had no plan that we would.

We waited in the Holding area to collect our two posters. We said goodbye to Scott whom we got to know quite well. A production team member gave us a souvenir bag. There is more information under the "Behind The Scenes" section.

Glimpses of Our Props
(Preliminary Poster Design)

Proposed Life Card Ideas – Approved by our producer and not approved by the production team

Proposed T-Shirt for the Dragons – Not approved by our producer

Proposed T-Shirt – Approved by our producer (for Nelson only and not to be distributed to the Dragons)

Beth's Dress – Approved by our producer

Posters – Approved by our producer

Premiere

PREMIERE

After our studio taping, we thought we would stand a good chance to be aired (at least that's how we felt after our on-stage performance). We became the *Dragons' Den's* devoted fans and were patiently waiting for the new Season to be aired.

Once we knew the premiere date (2 October), we sat in front of our television for the first episode. Since we did not receive any notice (entrepreneurs would get at least a 2-week notice), we knew we would not be on the Premiere. Nevertheless, we enjoyed the pitches and were multi-tasking for the last few minutes (mostly commercials).

All of a sudden, we thought we recognized my voice. We saw the last glimpse of me chatting with Kevin and the episode ended. We froze and panicked as we never imagined we would be showcased at the end of the premiere. After recovering from this unexpected surprise, we rewound the episode (great that we programmed our recorder to record the whole episode) and figured out what's going on.

You may laugh at us that we actually watched the last 10 minutes of the Premiere unlimited times. First, we had to recall what happened as it had been over six solid months since our studio visit. Second, we wanted to count the number of pitchers on the preview and started the countdown to estimate our Showtime. We lost track how often we watched it and kept that premiere episode in our TV recorder for months.

For our first Den experience, we were very fortunate that part of our pitch was on the premiere when they showcased future episodes. It was a guarantee that our pitch would be aired and "when" was the only unknown factor.

As time passed by, we got more used to the program rundown. We figured out that one or two of the previewed entrepreneurs were on each episode. When it got to the last few entrepreneurs in December and the show paused for the holidays, we knew that ours would be aired early the following year.

It was no big surprise (still an exciting moment though) when we received an email notice from a production associate on 20 December confirming our pitch would be aired on 22 January 2014. Our Den experience was a time and labor-intensive process. It took close to a year from Start to End; that is, it took from our auditions on 7 February 2013 to see our episode aired on 22 January 2014.

Prep Before Showtime

Remember we would not have access to our production tape. The best we could get would be an in-house recording on our pitch when it was aired in January.

Another option was the web version which would become available online on the CBC Dragons' Den portal approximately 24 hours after the air date. What could we offer to the media if they would like to write an article on our Den experience?

We had the following available:
- Audition photos
- Pre and Post-pitching photos at the studio especially the photo took by a production associate minutes before we visited the Den
- Four on-stage production photos which we received in the email notice

Note: The email notice also came with a copy of the *Dragons' Den* Fall 2013 Release and two sample templates which we could use and modify for our emails to the media.

Upon receipt of the email notice, I started following cbcdragonsden on Twitter and provided the production associate with our website and social media handles as follows:

- Twitter Handle (fiedlerbeth)
- Facebook Page (fiedlerbeth)
- Website (ezcolortrading.com)

We also started knocking at over 10 different media doors in October (when we were showcased at the Premiere). A few responded asking us to touch base with them again when we had the exact air date. Our story ended up gaining some exposure in two newspapers (inclusive of their online portals) in January 2014.

As a result of our story appearing in *The Hamilton Spectator* on 6 January, we received an email from a professor at McMaster University. He invited us to do a presentation to his Entrepreneur evening students. We accepted his suggestion and shared some investment tips with his students (close to 100) on 15 January.

Season VIII Production Photos (Source: CBC Television)

thespec.com on 5 January 2014

Jan 05, 2014 | Vote 0 0

How Beth broke free from her trading addiction

By Lisa Marr

Beth Fiedler is something of a recovering day trader.

She used to wake before the markets opened in London, England, at 2:30 a.m., then would check in on the U.S. markets around 9 a.m. before she'd take a half-hour break at noon and then check markets until four when they closed.

Then the Asian market would open at 6 p.m. and she'd watch that until about 11 p.m. when she'd go to bed.

Then get up again for the 2:30 a.m. markets in London.

Then she'd collapse. Again and again.

"My doctor told me I had to stop, I had to

Fiedlers
Handout
The Fiedlers, Beth and Nelson of Hamilton, will be on the Dragons Den later in January.

The Hamilton Spectator on 6 January 2014

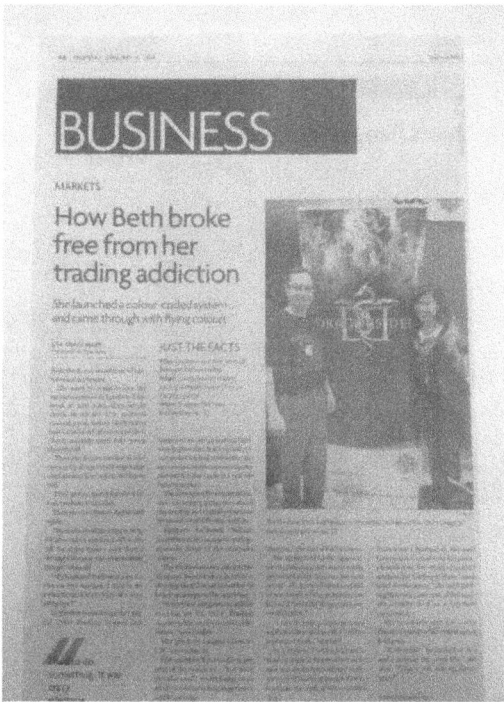

37

The Record on 21 January 2014

Local day-trading educational business enters Dragons' Den

By Rose Simone

CAMBRIDGE — A local couple who sell their own day-trading system will have their pitch to start a day-trading online learning academy aired on the *Dragons' Den* television program.

Beth and Nelson Fiedler of EZ Color Trading in Cambridge pitched their business idea to the dragons on the CBC show almost a year ago. It will air on Wednesday at 8 p.m.

"It was a special life experience for both of us," said Beth Fiedler, an immigrant from Hong Kong who designed a day-trading tool with a colour-coded system of indicators she selected based on her experience to help traders predict the ups and downs of the markets.

Traders, mostly in the United States, lease her system on a monthly

Dragons Den
CBC Television
Cambridge couple Beth and Nelson Fiedler of EZ Color Trading make their pitch to the dragons on the CBC Television show, Dragons' Den.

subscription basis. The couple also sells a number of educational resources for day traders on the firm's website. Beth has also written a book, *My Roller Coaster Ride*, that describes her own ups and downs and exhaustive days and nights spent obsessing about futures trading.

Showtime

SHOWTIME

One Take (In Or Out)

We waited for almost a year for our pitch to be aired. It was finally here on 22 January 2014. Words cannot express how we felt. We had been keeping the outcome of our presentation to us for months. After our pitch was aired, we were free to talk and could tell others what happened in the Den.

We had our air date, but we did not know the exact time. A typical episode consists of five to six pitches. We patiently did our countdown. First ... Second ... Third ...

Ours was the preview of the third pitch, meaning ours would be the next after some commercials. Our hearts raced. Our hands sweated. Our heads spun.

I was also paying close attention to the two Twitter accounts (cbcdragonsden and fiedlerbeth). I re-tweeted a few and wrote a few tweets at the appropriate moment. From the tweets, I learned that Arlene has a soft spot for songs. She often cannot help laughing.

After our taping, we did ask Scott why the Dragons could not hold their laughter for the first few minutes. He told us it could be the leftover effect of the former pitch.

He could not disclose more specific information and we understood.

The Cat Out Of The Bag

If our readers missed our pitch on 22 January, there were no worries. It's available online 24/7 on the CBC Dragons' Den website (Season VIII, Episode 13). We felt proud because we accomplished the following:

- Nelson did his magic trick flawlessly
- We stayed cool and focused throughout the whole presentation (regardless of the Dragons' reaction)
- We made two of the Dragons (Arlene and Kevin) cry in front of millions
- We shared our passion and message with millions (our message to both inexperienced and experienced investors: you need a solid foundation on trading discipline, capital protection, money management and risk/reward ratio before doing an investment of any kind)

Our proposal was about helping investors not to lose money. The first and foremost important question that investors should ask themselves is about not losing money. In the real world, most products and service providers talk about how they can help their customers make money. They downplay the importance of financial literacy and money management.

I have learned the hard way, ie investing in years of time and thousands of losing trades. I am still thankful for the Den opportunity. The Dragons' opt-out did not stop me.

Post-Pitch

We were released from the Consent Agreement and could talk freely about our experience. We did not contact any media after our pitch was aired. Why? I guess we were on an exploratory and reactive stage to see if there might be potential investors or partners who would be interested in our business idea.

We understood that the portion being aired did not really provide enough details on our idea that might arouse potential investors/partners' interest. For example, what (the proposal and revenue projection), who (target audience), how (format, terms, rundown, operation and premises), when (timeline), and where (online portal). It did not hurt to hope that there could be visionary investors who could see what we might have left out.

So what actually happened after our pitch was aired? We got a few emails and most did not stick. I responded to all of them yet there were no follow-ups. We received two nasty tweets. Of course we ignored them and stayed positive. I did not choose to respond. Silence is golden.

We were looked down upon by some who did not appreciate the efforts we spent and the challenges we encountered. Luckily they were strangers on the street and not in our circle of friends and partners. We did not need to deal with them at a personal or professional level.

To look at it positively, we were recognized by some on the street who praised our courage and recognized the efforts we made to get that far.

To be turned down by the Dragons and seeing our pitch not edited the way we would have liked did bruise our ego. However, it was an amazing life experience. We took the challenge, learned from it and moved on.

Guess who had a bigger ego? Your guess is right. He felt disappointed because his magic trick was cut. I could feel his frustration and that explained why his role was more proactive in our second chance presentation. Having said that, I understood the time constraint and appreciated the efforts spent in editing our 15-minute presentation to a 6-minute one.

Our egos were bruised a little. We recovered shortly and stayed positive and focused again. Without the Dragons as our EZ Color Trading Academy partners, how could I share what I learned from my Futures journey?

Months after our episode (April), I started writing my two years Future experiences. I stayed with the original book idea and named my book "My Roller Coaster Ride".

What's Next?

Season 9?

Passion

WHAT'S NEXT

We were barking up the wrong tree. What's next? We resumed where we left off and went back to our daily routine. I started writing bits and pieces of my Futures experiences on some scrap paper.

Without knowing, I spent some hours every week in front of the computer and recalled what I encountered when I was learning how to day trade Futures. Starting in April 2013, I entered a weekly calendar item to remind me to write at least 25 pages every two weeks up until July. It was my plan to have my book available by August.

I went through emails to locate the publishing package which was purchased in December 2011. I found the purchase information and confirmed with the publishing vendor that my package was still valid. It was a basic black&white publishing package for a 6"x9" paperback.

I had a few slip ups on my writing schedule. When I finally caught up, I was overwhelmed with 300 typed pages on my hands. They were chronological yet I did not have a clue on how to organize them into a book.

Putting it aside did clear my head. I started drafting out a list of chapter names. Then marked my 300 pages with the chapter or chapters they most likely belonged to. It took a week to do back-and-forth categorization. Once I completed the manual sorting of papers or should I say chapters and was happy with their flow, I worked on the electronic version on my computer.

I spent the last week of August proofreading my book 10 more times (likely to be more) before finalizing the publishing process with a US publishing company on 28 August. You could imagine my joy when I received my first proof copy in September.

Unexpected Roadblocks

Life is always full of challenges. I experienced a few when I tried to sell my book on consignment. I learned about a common practice: almost all bookstores ask for a 45% discount off the retail price. I would be sponsoring $5 per copy sold.

It did not make sense to me. In order to lower my publishing cost which was about $15/copy, I explored self-publishing. My self-publishing venture could be my next book. To make the story short, I created a new cover, made slight changes to my book, and self-published my Ride book in November.

Pride & Joy

Did I ever dream of writing a book? No.

Did I ever dream of self-publishing a book? No.

Did I ever plan to return to the Den for a second chance presentation? No.

Upon completion of the first few book signing, I knew why I spent so much time and effort in sharing my experience on the Ride book. Having encountered what I experienced for two long years in the Futures world, I wanted others not to make the same mistakes which could cost them both years and thousands of dollars.

Jim
Mike
Beth
Arlene Nelson
Vikram
Dragons
David
Fiedler's
IX
Season
CBC
Den
The

Audition

AUDITION

With the new "My Roller Coaster Ride" book copies on hand (a physical commodity) plus a book signing schedule (to prove our diligence), we were in a better position to win the Dragons this round. We started watching out for the Season IX auditions schedule.

When the auditions schedule was released in early January 2014, I submitted an online submission on 9 January. We had close to a month to prepare for our audition on 6 February at the Holiday Inn in Burlington.

Prep for Audition

Back to the most important element of a presentation. How could we make an impactful introduction for the first 10 seconds? We also had other questions such as

Did we need to alert the audition producers that it was our second chance? Would there be a different audition schedule for second chance entrepreneurs?

Luckily, we had some CBC production contacts who we could ask. We found out second chance entrepreneurs would have to go through exactly the same audition procedures as the first chance pitchers. However, we should identify ourselves as a second chance entrepreneur if the producers did not recognize us. Most did because the production team went through all pitches together when they did editing and screening.

For the first two weeks, I was haunted with sensible and non-sensible prop ideas that could make an impactful introduction. For example,

- Wore masks to create suspense (because of our second chance status)
- Sang one or two lines of the EZ Color Trading Academy song while walking down to the Den (might trigger an instant connection with the Dragons)
- Used some roller coaster statistics to engage the Dragons in a Q&A format
- Brought in a real roller coaster set (a physical object to illustrate the ups and downs I experienced)

Nelson reacted strongly to the first two ideas. He worried that singing would put the Dragons into a laughing loop again. I agreed to drop the singing idea. Wearing a mask was not a sensible choice because the Dragons might not take us seriously again. On second thought, a mask might ruin my eye makeup too.

Finding some roller coaster statistics was easy. It took me less than an hour to get relevant and interesting data that we could use for our presentation. The only challenge left? A physical roller coaster set that was big enough for a television show and we could physically manage its transportation from our home to the audition venue.

At that stage, we did not worry about its transportation to the downtown CBC studio. First things first, and that was passing the audition screening and be shortlisted for taping. I visited several online stores to find a suitable roller coaster set. I located a good candidate (from a US toy portal) and placed an order for less than US$25 (came with free shipping).

The roaster coaster set arrived within a week and I spent about four hours assembling it. It was my first and likely to be the last roller coaster set that I assembled. I was proud of my masterpiece and posted a video clip to my Facebook account.

Budget Control

We needed to maintain the same budget management for our second round. I spent less than $40 for our props, namely

- Roller coaster set ($30 after US$/C$ conversion)
- Black foam-core board ($5)
- Color print of a poster ($5)

Rehearsal – Rehearsal - Rehearsal

Our business presentation was about a book "My Roller Coaster Ride". It was my real-life experience. It was about trading discipline, capital protection and not losing money. Our Ask: $20,000 in exchange for 30% of our books' proceeds and 20% perpetuity after money is recouped. We stayed with the same Ask for our presentation to the Dragons.

I'm not sure if it was because of our first pitch experience, but we felt quite at ease for our audition preparation. We originally thought we would need to rent a van or truck for the roller coaster set. Then we figured out our car was big enough without causing any substantial damage to the set. We removed a 4" red pole from the set and were prepared to do some last-minute fixes to any loose nuts and bolts.

It was a great relief that we figured out an easy way to transport it. Once that was done, we spent our last few nights on polishing our presentation.

I almost forgot I spent additional time learning more about the publishing industry. I read many blogs about self-publishing and existing channels for book fairs and exhibits.

Second Chance Audition

We got up at 6:00 am and reached the venue around 8:00 am. We were the first ones at the atrium where the audition would be held at 11:00 am to 6:00 pm. We left the roller coaster set in the car and found an exit to bring in our props when the audition started. We also found a portable luggage cart with a hanging cloth covering our props.

We spent the first hour rehearsing our presentation. There was a hotel staff who recognized us as she watched our first pitch on 22 January. Her kind words and compliments did boost our spirit. She appreciated our efforts to get that far. We thanked her for her support and she would watch out for our second chance performance.

Priscilla and Rich were in charge of the auditions with a few associates (volunteers) helping out the check-in and distribution of Consent & Release Forms. We brought along a hard copy of our online submission form so that we did not need to complete a submission form on the spot. Both producers recognized us as they saw our pitch a few weeks ago.

Once the producers got the audition stage ready (the other end of the atrium) while the entrepreneurs waited close to the other side, we were asked to present our second chance pitch.

We uncovered our props and delivered our second chance presentation smoothly. We addressed their raised questions on how to use the investment money, our revenue projection and the estimated return on investment.

Upon completion, both producers shook our hand. Rich asked us if he could take a photo with us. Of course, we were delighted to have our photo taken. We finished our pitch around 1:00 pm.

Guess the benefits of being an early bird for an audition? A great time saver! Had time to calm down our nerves. Threw in a few rehearsals with ease.

We got to the venue three hours before the audition schedule. There were about 10-12 entrepreneurs around 11:00 am. When we finished, there were at least 40 entrepreneurs in the waiting area.

Post-Audition

After our audition, we both felt great that we would stand a good chance to be invited back to the studio for taping. We heard nothing in early March and started having doubts.

For Season VIII, we got a call and an email notice on 26 February. We were using the same timeline for the second chance pitchers. We got an unofficial update that the production team had not decided if they would have a second chance episode for Season IX. They would make a decision before mid-March.

On 13 March, we received a phone call from Scott confirming our second chance taping on 12 April. He would be our producer giving us guidance on our pitch preparation. He would like to receive our script and rehearsal video in two weeks.

Photo Time Before Audition.

Being Recognized As Second Chance Pitchers

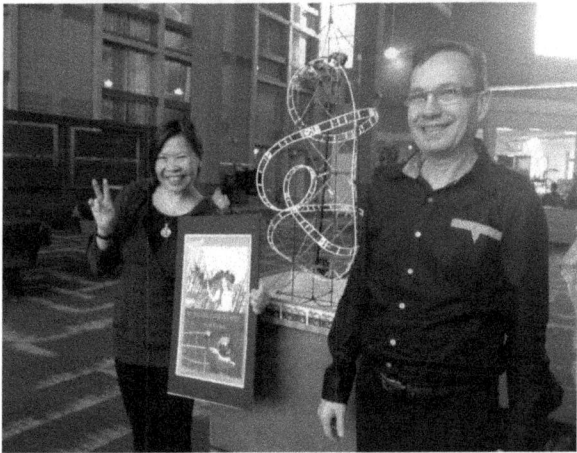

Glimpses Of Our Audition Props (Multilanguage Poster)

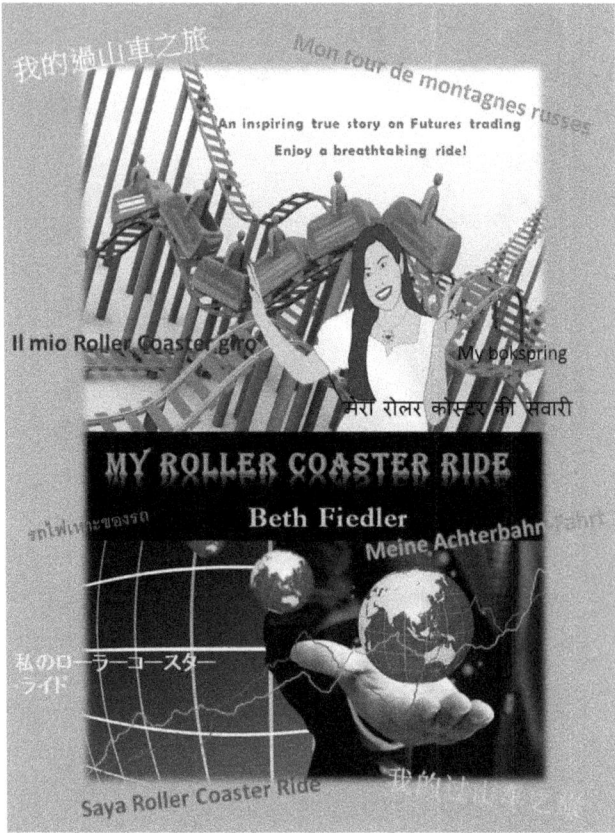

Book Copies of My Roller Coaster Ride (self-publishing version)

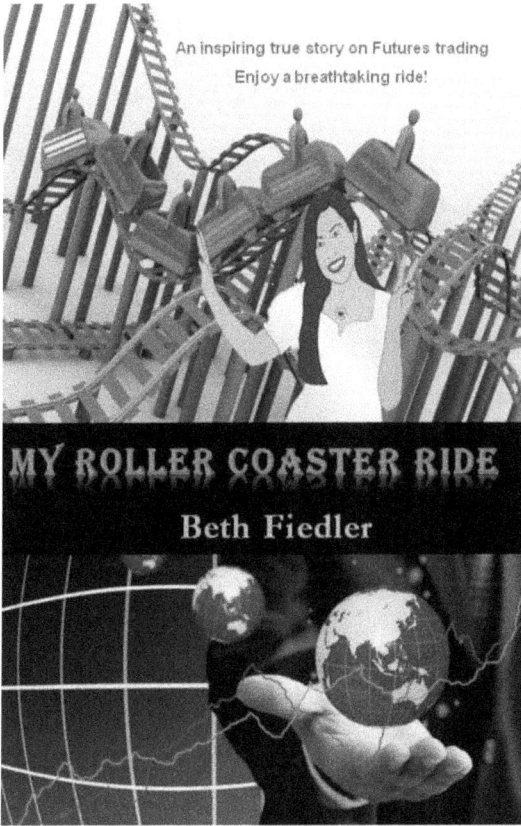

An inspiring true story on Futures trading
Enjoy a breathtaking ride!

MY ROLLER COASTER RIDE

Beth Fiedler

Copy of My Roller Coaster Ride (first version)

Props Rehearsal Rundown — Second Chance

SECOND CHANCE

Preparation Of Season IX Pitch

Season IX Dragons:

Arlene Dickinson
David Chilton
Jim Treliving
Michael Wekerle
Vikram Vij

I used the same *Dragons' Den* 2013 Pitcher Guide to prepare our second chance presentation. To be second chance presenters, we enjoyed the following pros and cons:

Pros

We knew the flow with minimal uncertainties. We partnered with the same producer who had faith and confidence in us. We could count on Scott to provide us with insightful suggestions and support.

Cons

We had to find creative ways to stand out as we would be dealing with the same Dragons who chose to opt-out last time. It would be critical to add more dynamics and entertainment elements to our presentation so that our pitch would be aired regardless of the outcome.

Pitch Preparation

We had Scott's endorsement on our audition script except with a more interesting opening. A physical roller coaster set was eye-catching yet it was an unknown factor. Its operation sound must be tested and approved at the set.

First, we planned to have a portrait banner on an X-display stand (instead of a poster). Our idea was not approved. Instead, Scott suggested that we use a poster as before.

On 16 March, we learned about the departure of two Dragons (Kevin and Bruce). Once we recovered from our first reaction, I did research on the two new Dragons (Mike and Vikram). It was challenging to get their photos for my poster design. I ended up using the ones I found online. Scott approved my design because of the printing timeline.

After a few phone consultation chats with Scott, we decided to add a last-minute pregnancy element to the introduction on 9 April (2 days before taping). I contacted several pregnancy stores inclusive of hospitals to explore an option to buy or borrow a fake belly. I had no luck and I created mine using a fleecy scarf and safety pins. It must look real and big enough to accommodate a copy of my book.

Our neighbors Jen and Alfred were helpful in giving me comments on the belly shape and how a pregnant lady should walk. On 11 April evening, we had a winner.

Please refer to the Behind The Scenes section for the pre-pitch activities.

Pitch Time

A production team member brought us to the top of the stairs and asked us to wait for the countdown before descending into the Den.

Nelson carried two posters. We got to the presentation spots (where the two Xs were) and asked the Dragons to give us a few minutes for set up. Nelson set up the posters on the easel (with the back exposing to the Dragons). He turned on the roller coaster set.

We successfully delivered an interesting twist with my book inside a fake belly. Nelson gave out book copies to the Dragons with a tailor-made bookmark with the Dragon's home language (if applicable). For example,

- Arlene (Afrikaans)
- David (French)
- Jim (English)
- Mike (Chinese)
- Vikram (Hindi)

Nelson adopted Mike's habitual hand movement into his performance. We covered what we wanted to cover before addressing their raised questions in the Q&A session. Arlene read out my biography and complimented my accomplishments. She also kept asking me to sing again.

Mike is the only Dragon with solid merchant banking experience. David is the Dragon who wrote books about investment. It was normal that the other Dragons stayed on the sidelines. Jim was the first Dragon who chose to opt-out.

Arlene asked Mike to give me three investment related questions. I had no clue about the first two questions as I did not encounter them in my Futures journey. The last one was about capital protection which I preached about in my book. Every single investment must have a pair of profit target and stop loss orders to protect one's capital.

Mike was out because he is the only Dragon who did not have a book. He would write one and conflict of interest was his opt-in reason.

Arlene and David were out because they opined Futures trading was a high-risk financial instrument. Vikram was out because he was on a roller coaster ride. We thanked the Dragons for their time and left the Den.

Post-Pitch Update

Let's pause here to remind the readers that our business idea was a book on a trader's real-life story. It was a book about not losing money. It was a book with a mission to remind investors from different walks of life the importance of trading discipline, capital protection and money management.

I estimated that the Dragons had focused on the wrong premise when assessing our proposal. We were not encouraging high-risk investment. On the contrary, we shared our trading mistakes in the book. We gave the readers constructive recommendations about how to safeguard falling into trading traps.

It was very unfortunate that we were unable to steer the conversation back to the mission of the book. We are again barking up the wrong tree. Most lost their vision that a financial literacy movement (in whatever form) could be helpful to most people.

We have no regrets that we visited the Den a second time. Scott met us at the Den exit with his production team. He asked us how we felt and what would be our next move. We told him we would continue educating investors about the importance of capital protection.

"My Roller Coaster Ride" has been available online (in over 50 countries) since August 2013. We retired the original version and replaced it with a second edition in August 2014.

Poster Design (Before The Dragon Change Announcement)

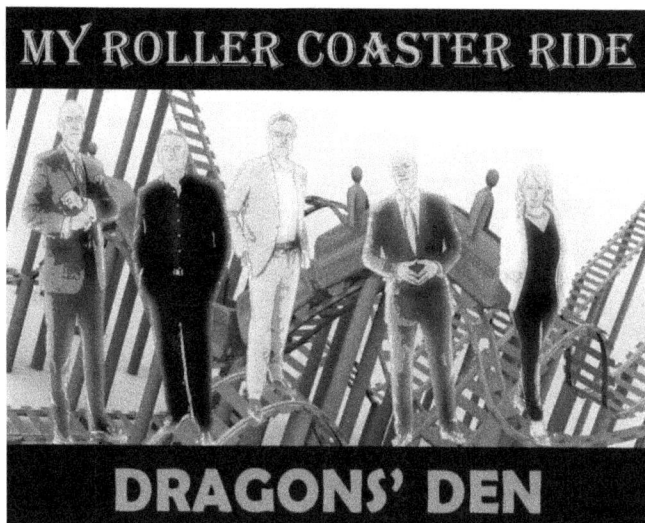

Poster Design With New Dragons

Poster Design with New Dragons Plus Their Autographs

Bookmarks For The Dragons

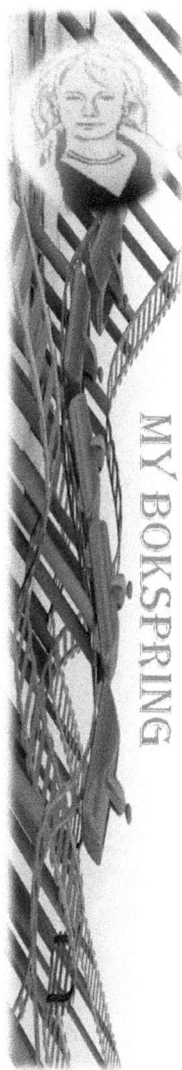

MY ROLLER COASTER RIDE

我的過山車之旅

MY BOKSPRING

Bookmarks For The Dragons (Continued)

MON TOUR DE MONTAGNES RUSSES

मेरा रोलर कोस्टर की सवारी

Unexpected
Twist

UNEXPECTED TWIST

When we did not receive an email notice about our air date in mid-December, I started doing research into the past few second chance episodes. The second chance episode was aired on the first Wednesday of January for the past two seasons. I estimated that shortlisted second chance entrepreneurs should have received their email notice by or before 12 December.

To resolve the uncertainty that had been haunting us for weeks, we made an effort to locate the 3 December episode, which was the last original one before the holidays, and watched the episodes on 14 December. We held our breath when we got to the preview of the second chance pitchers. We were not there. To us, it was sad and disheartening. However, we had closure.

To Nelson, it was a blow. His second chance performance was exceptional. He incorporated our producer's last-minute suggestion into our pitch flawlessly. He demonstrated competence in managing the Dragons' raised questions. He even imitated one of the Dragons' habitual hand movements and established an instant connection with him. As of this moment, I am still proud of my hubby's on-stage performance.

To me, not being on the second chance preview or the second chance episode was a relief. I could still feel the embarrassment when most of the Dragons could not hold their laughter for our first presentation.

On the morning of 15 December, I tried to connect with our producer to confirm that we would not be among the cut-and-paste section on the second chance episode. He was not available so I planned to try again in the afternoon.

At 1:41 pm, I received an email confirmation from a production associate confirming our pitch will be featured as their ninth web pitch of Dragons' Den Season IX on 8 January 2015 (Thursday). Originally I thought there was an inadvertent typo on the date as the show has always been on a Wednesday.

Upon receipt of the email, I immediately called our producer Scott. He was not available, and I left him a thank you message. I knew Nelson would be thrilled. It took me additional efforts to stay silent when Nelson called me a few times in the afternoon. I was waiting to see his WOW moment.

I took my time to share the email with Nelson. Then I realized our pitch would be released as a web pitch and not part of a regular episode on the television.

The email notice came with four production photos, a copy of the *Dragons' Den* Season Press Release Final, and two sample letters to the press. They recommended that we join the Den discussion on the event date; it was also suggested that we followed them on twitter @cbcdragon, and used the hashtag #cbcdragonsden to add more interest in our pitch.

I confirmed receipt of their email and provided the required social media information as follows:

- Twitter Handle (fiedlerbeth)
- Facebook Page (fiedlerbeth)
- Website (bethfiedler.com)

I had some email exchanges with the production associate to confirm our web pitch. It would be released around 12:00 noon on 8 January 2014 (Thursday). I updated our websites with the production photos and pitch release information.

Season IX Production Photos (Source: CBC Television)

Web Pitch

WEB PITCH

Countdown again. What an amazing start for the New Year! We were honored that our pitch was selected to be the ninth featured web pitch.

We learned that our web pitch would be released in the afternoon on 8 January 2015 (Thursday). The production associate has recommended us to login to our Twitter account and follow the cbcdragonsden tweets closely.

As mentioned in the Second Chance section, we delivered a special introduction (with my book in a "fake" belly) to make a dynamic entrance with entertaining elements. We had a roller coaster on stage while engaging the Dragons with interesting statistical questions right at the beginning.

We had a physical product created out of hard work not to mention thousands of hours spent accumulating the knowledge shared about the book. We missed the fact that most of the Dragons knew nothing about Futures trading.

Three of the Dragons were present for our first Den visit. They might have had a biased judgment on our second proposal and failed to realize the value our book would bring to those who would appreciate sharing a real trader's story.

Mike has outstanding credentials on the trading floor and merchant banking. We thought he could be a good fit. When the questions he threw to us were more institutional investor-related, we knew then he could not relate to our mission on educating retail investors. I guess it was a valid opt-out reason that he would be writing a book about investment.

While Vikram was the only Dragon who has self-publishing experience, it could be challenging for him to partner with us in a completely different arena. His expertise has been on dining and cuisines.

If you watched our pitch, you can tell we were taken aback by the Dragons' questions because most of them were not about our book's distribution channels, revenue projection and proposed marketing activities.

Our book is an easy read for those who would like to learn how to safeguard investment mishaps. We respected the Dragons' decision. We recognized we had different mindsets and carried no grudge against any of the Dragons.

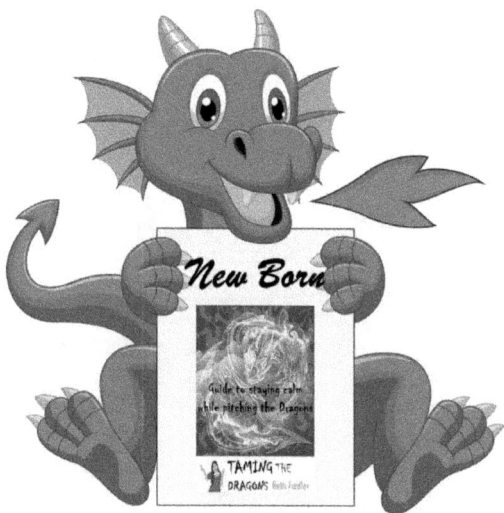

NEW BORN

Does every cloud have a silver lining? We visited the Den not once, but twice. For both visits, we thought we would bring home a deal. For our second chance, we could smell success once we got a taping invitation.

We learned that there were about 15 second chance entrepreneurs for the season. We thought we would be one of the winners who would get a deal. Actually, we visualized that the Dragons would fight for the opportunity to partner with us on promoting financial literacy.

Yes, we were wrong. Our egos were bruised substantially. We talked a lot to release our tension and grievances. Out of the blue, I visited my favorite portal and searched for "fire dragon" graphics. I was thrilled to locate one that talked to me. Without my knowing, the first "Taming The Dragons" book cover design was born in August 2014.

I used the same strategy for this new book once I made a decision about its size and estimated number of pages. I had a bi-weekly calendar item up to early December. I used the month of December for final cover design, editing, and proofreading.

What did I want to accomplish by writing "Taming The Dragons"? It will always serve to remind us to give our best shot in life. There is no "if" unless and until we give it a try. That way we will not have any regrets. If it does not work out, let go and move on.

Do we care about others' feedback on our Den visits and performances? We did. No more. We went far enough to learn from these two once in a lifetime experiences.

What does this book offer to the readers? It shows the readers two real-life journeys for those who always wonder what motivated some entrepreneurs to visit the Den. For those who want to learn more about the application process, auditions and taping, I certainly hope that this book will fulfill their curiosity.

Behind The Scenes

BEHIND THE SCENES

For our first pitch, we were part of the afternoon batch 12:00 noon to 5:00 pm. We arrived at the CBC Studio building (John Street entrance) around 11:00 am and registered at the check-in table.

There were about ten entrepreneurs (both individuals and groups) at the check-in area. When it was around 12:30 pm, some production team members checked our names on their list and gave us *Dragons' Den* stickers to put on our clothing for access identification. We also received two copies of the Consent & Release Form which had to be signed and returned to our producer before our presentation.

They divided us into groups (one to two entrepreneurs per group) and we took turns taking an elevator to the staging area on the 10th floor. We were assigned a table (approximately 2' x 4') with our business name or idea on it. We were told to unpack our presentation materials and props. We left them on the table for a logistics walk-through with our producer who would join us shortly.

Our producer Scott arrived at our table within minutes. We returned our signed Consent & Release Form copies to him. He told us a group of producers would briefly go over all our props. He would do a quick introduction about our business proposal. Nelson might be asked to do his magic trick and it was the same for my introduction song. We would need to adapt and consider their suggested changes. Our pitch would be the second last one of the day. We would have time to do more rehearsals with him before taping.

The producers came to our table. Scott went through our props and business idea. Nelson practiced his magic trick in front of them. They loved his performance. I sang the introduction. As I had a soft voice, the director asked me to move two steps closer to the Dragons before singing my lines.

Scott assured us that there would be an easel in the Den for Nelson to position the two posters. Considering my soft voice, he would alert the audio technician to adjust my microphone accordingly.

Nelson asked Scott how we could make our entrance more dynamic so that we would stand a better chance to be aired. He suggested waving to the Dragons from the windows. No one has done it before. We both thought it was a good idea. He gave us further instructions as to when and where to pause and wave to the Dragons.

After all entrepreneurs met with the producers, the floor director took us for a tour of the *Dragons' Den* set. He explained the rules and procedures. For example,

- The two designated presentation spots (X) on the studio floor located approximately five meters (15 feet) from the Dragons. If the entrepreneurs stray from these presentation spots without prior approval, they would be interrupted by the floor director during their presentation.
- All presenters must remain standing during the pitch unless otherwise approved by their producer before taping.

- For those who got their producer's approval to hand out gift bags or packages to the Dragons, they would start with the Dragons on the right.

- He also reminded us that generally no more than one or two Dragons will be allowed to leave their chairs at one time. Be prepared that one or all Dragons may refuse to participate in a requested activity. Also one or multiple Dragons would want to test or try a product without being asked.

Last but not least, the floor director assured us that all pre-approved logistics (such as a table, cloth and an easel) would be on-stage for the presenters.

After the Den tour, we returned to our assigned table and waited patiently for our turn. A production assistant visited us and took a photo for us. When there were three entrepreneurs left for taping, we were escorted to a snack lounge with light refreshments such as coffee and donuts.

We went out to the corridor area. Scott and Katie did a few rounds of rehearsal with us. They were impressed by our smooth presentation and diligence in addressing their mock questions. They reminded us that it was extremely important to be in control most of the time especially before the Q&A session.

It was almost 4:15 pm when two pitches were left. Scott told us the pitch before us took more time to clear the stage. They could only accommodate one more pitch (that would be ours) if the Den could be available within the next few minutes. It was a disappointment to the entrepreneurs after us. They waited for over five hours and were asked to return the next morning.

We were back to the "on deck" lounge for last-minute hair and makeup touch-ups. An audio technician attached a wireless microphone to us. We would know in a few minutes if our pitch would be taped that day.

Two camera crew members were near-by and they took some photos for us. They even interviewed us asking us a few questions.

Scott came over around 4:30 pm confirming our pitch would be on. He wished us good luck and told us he would be waiting for us right outside the Den exit. A production assistant brought us into the studio and did a quick microphone level check. A production team member brought us to the top of the stairs and asked us to wait for the countdown before descending into the Den.

5...4...3...2...1... Pitch Time!

Season IX Start To Finish (Very similar to our Season VIII experience with slight differences)

For our second pitch, we were part of the afternoon batch again. This round we knew more about the neighborhood and it took Nelson minutes to park. We registered at the check-in table at the lobby area (John Street entrance) around 11:00 am.

There were about ten entrepreneurs (both individuals and groups) at the check-in area. When it was around 12:00 noon, some production team members checked our names on their list and gave us a *Dragons' Den* sticker to put on our clothing for access identification. We also received two copies of the Consent & Release Form which had to be signed and returned to our producer before our presentation.

We got a luggage cart for our props (pre-arranged with our producer Scott) when it was time to take an elevator to the staging area on the 10th floor. We were assigned with a table (approximately 2' x 4') with EZ Color Trading on it. We were told to unpack our presentation materials and props. We left them on the table for a logistics walk-through with our producer who would join us shortly.

Our producer Scott arrived at our table within minutes. We returned our signed Consent & Release Form copies to him. He told us a group of producers would briefly go over all our props. He would do a quick introduction on our business proposal. We would need to adapt and consider their suggested changes. Our pitch would likely be the third one. We would have time to do more rehearsals with him before taping.

The producers came to our table. Scott went through our props and business idea. They recognized us and we were like old friends chatting a little and they wished us good luck.

Scott assured us that there would be an easel in the Den for Nelson to position the two posters. He would also arrange to have our roller coaster set on stage at the appropriate position.

After all entrepreneurs met with the producers, the floor director took us for a tour of the *Dragons' Den* set. Katie was the floor director (who did our first auditions plus helping out our rehearsal for our first pitch). She explained the rules and procedures. For example,

- The two designated presentation spots (X) on the studio floor located approximately five meters (15 feet) from the Dragons. If the entrepreneurs stray from these presentation spots without prior approval, they would be interrupted by the floor director during their presentation.
- All presenters must remain standing during the pitch unless otherwise approved by their producer before taping.
- For those who got their producer's approval to hand out gift bags or packages to the Dragons, they would start with the Dragons on the right.
- She also reminded us that generally no more than one or two Dragons will be allowed to leave their chairs at one time. Be prepared that one or all Dragons may refuse to participate in a requested activity. Also one or multiple Dragons would want to test or try a product without being asked.

After the Den tour, we returned to our assigned table and did more rehearsals in front of Scott. Scott apologized for not spending too much time with us this round because he was being promoted from an associate producer to a producer after Season VIII. Producers' accountabilities were more on the production and not working directly with the entrepreneurs at a pitch level.

Our pitch was the only pitch he was coaching this season. We thanked him for doing that for us. We rehearsed a few times in front of Scott and he gave us amazing tips on how to make our performance more impactful.

It was quite challenging to adopt the suggested changes within minutes. Yes literally minutes because the first afternoon pitch was already on the set. We must be prompt and quick to make it happen or else our on-stage performance could be a disaster.

We are still very grateful to Scott for sharing his production expertise with us. His devotion and care have made our Den experiences very special and memorable. We did not feel lost most of the time because he always addressed our raised issues promptly.

For our second studio visit, the entrepreneurs stayed at the staging area (our assigned table) most of the time. We were not escorted to a snack lounge like last time.

It was around 2:00 pm when Scott told us our pitch would be next. A production assistant visited our table and took a photo for us before we went to the "on deck" lounge for last-minute hair and makeup touch-ups. An audio technician attached a wireless microphone to us. Scott came over around 2:30 pm wished us good luck. He would be waiting for us right outside the Den exit.

A production assistant brought us into the studio and did a quick microphone level check. A production team member brought us to the top of the stairs and asked us to wait for the countdown before descending into the Den.

5…4…3…2…1… Pitch Time!

Season VIII CBC Studio (John Street, Toronto), Check-In Area

Season VIII Snack Lounge

Season VIII Souvenir Bag (The *Dragons' Den* Guide To Investor-Ready Business Plans, a mug, a photo frame with an instant photo taken before our pitch, and two certificates)

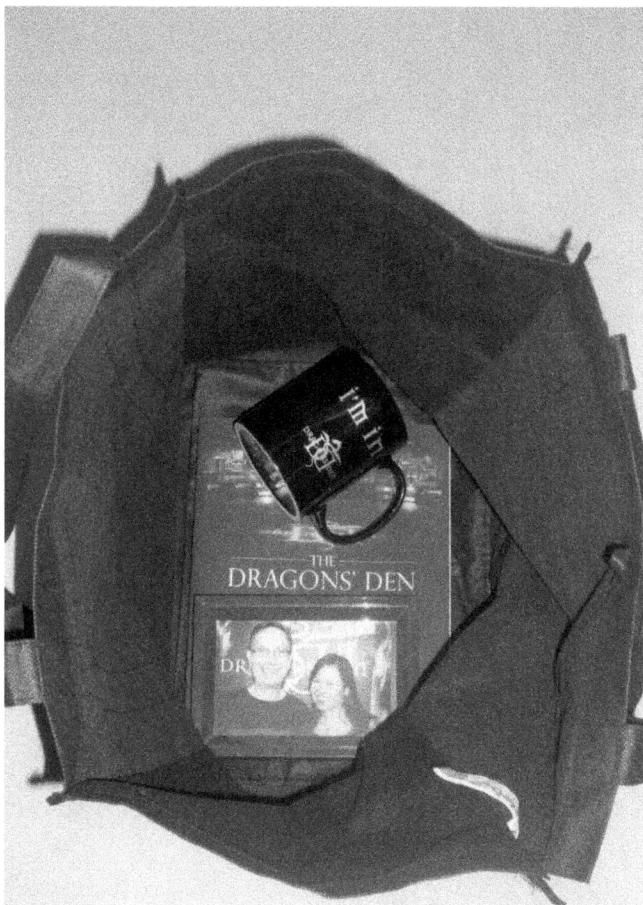

Closer Look At Our Souvenirs

Season VIII Certificates With An Inadvertent Typo On Our Last Name (should be Fiedler)

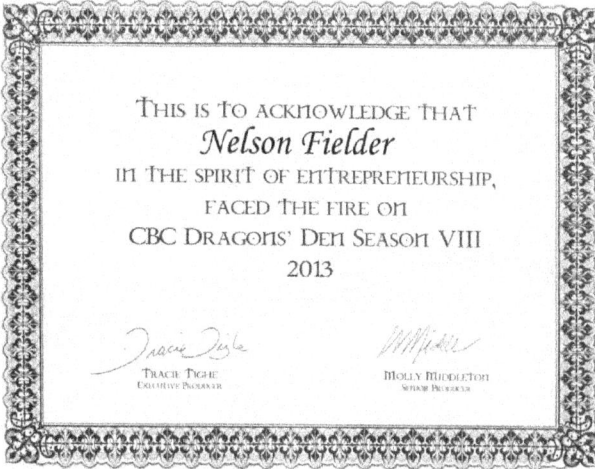

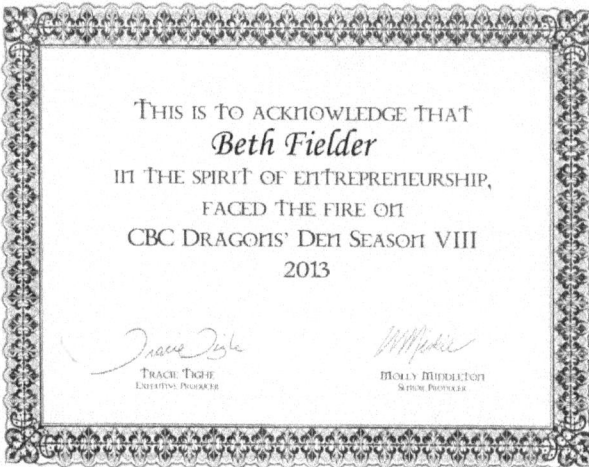

THIS IS TO ACKNOWLEDGE THAT
Nelson Fielder
IN THE SPIRIT OF ENTREPRENEURSHIP,
FACED THE FIRE ON
CBC DRAGONS' DEN SEASON VIII
2013

TRACIE TIGHE
EXECUTIVE PRODUCER

MOLLY MIDDLETON
SENIOR PRODUCER

THIS IS TO ACKNOWLEDGE THAT
Beth Fielder
IN THE SPIRIT OF ENTREPRENEURSHIP,
FACED THE FIRE ON
CBC DRAGONS' DEN SEASON VIII
2013

TRACIE TIGHE
EXECUTIVE PRODUCER

MOLLY MIDDLETON
SENIOR PRODUCER

Season VIII Certificates With The Correct Last Name

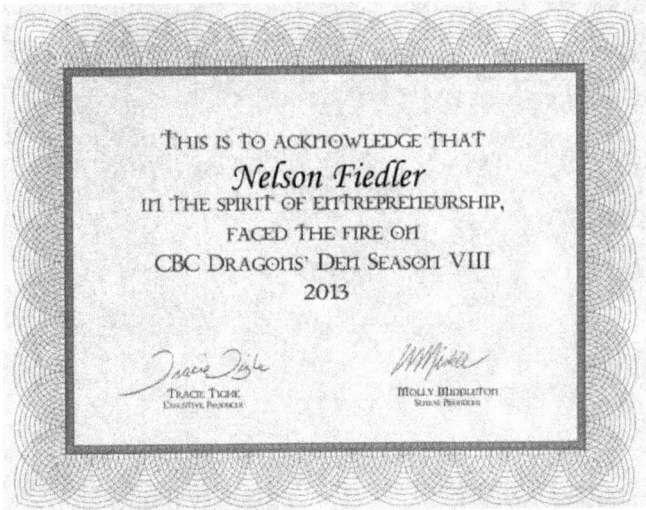

THIS IS TO ACKNOWLEDGE THAT

Nelson Fiedler

IN THE SPIRIT OF ENTREPRENEURSHIP,

FACED THE FIRE ON

CBC DRAGONS' DEN SEASON VIII

2013

TRACIE TIGHE
EXECUTIVE PRODUCER

MOLLY MIDDLETON
SENIOR PRODUCER

THIS IS TO ACKNOWLEDGE THAT

Beth Fiedler

IN THE SPIRIT OF ENTREPRENEURSHIP,

FACED THE FIRE ON

CBC DRAGONS' DEN SEASON VIII

2013

TRACIE TIGHE
EXECUTIVE PRODUCER

MOLLY MIDDLETON
SENIOR PRODUCER

Season IX Staging Area Pre-Pitch Photos

Season IX Staging Area Post-Pitch Photos

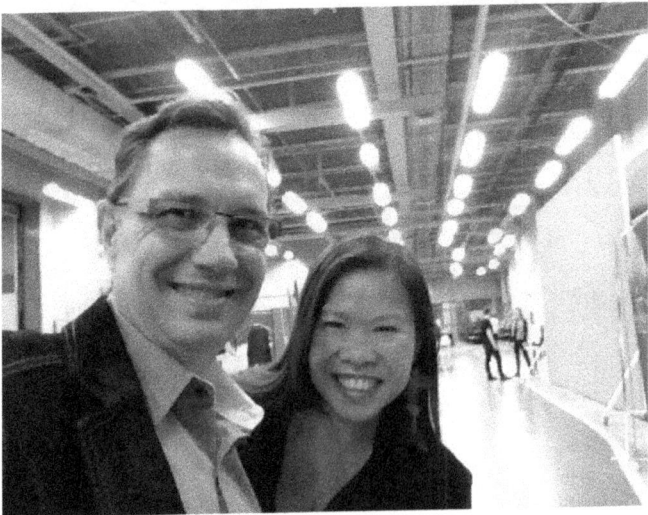

Season IX Souvenirs (A photo frame with an instant photo taken before our pitch and a $25 Boston Pizza gift card)

Season IX Certificates

THIS IS TO ACKNOWLEDGE THAT
Nelson Fiedler
IN THE SPIRIT OF ENTREPRENEURSHIP,
FACED THE FIRE ON
CBC DRAGONS' DEN SEASON IX
2014

TRACIE TIGHE
EXECUTIVE PRODUCER

AMY BOURNE
SENIOR PRODUCER

THIS IS TO ACKNOWLEDGE THAT
Beth Fiedler
IN THE SPIRIT OF ENTREPRENEURSHIP,
FACED THE FIRE ON
CBC DRAGONS' DEN SEASON IX
2014

TRACIE TIGHE
EXECUTIVE PRODUCER

AMY BOURNE
SENIOR PRODUCER

Do's &
Don'ts

DO'S & DON'TS

Having the opportunity to visit the Den two years in a row made us feel special. We shared our business ideas with seven Dragons (not five for most second chance entrepreneurs). That made us feel more special.

I mentioned a Consent & Release Form that must be signed by the entrepreneurs on different occasions. For example,

- Online application portal
- Auditions
- Taping at the CBC production studio

Those who did not sign the Consent & Release Form would not be eligible to participate in the auditions and/or pitching in front of the Dragons.

Now that I took care of the Consent & Release Form, let's go through the Do's and Don'ts.

Do's

All presentation materials and props must be pre-approved before reaching the CBC production studio. The entrepreneurs will not be compensated financially for any rejected materials. If for any reason, some of the props are not used for the presentation, the entrepreneurs will not be compensated financially for any unused materials.

When tabulating your company valuations, be sure to have qualitative and quantitative data to justify your Ask and company value. If the readers have a chance to view some former episodes, they would agree with me that almost all Dragons reacted strongly to entrepreneurs who overvalued their businesses. Fair value is one of the most important factors to make or break a deal.

Bear in mind that the Dragons will not be briefed or given any information about the entrepreneurs and their business ideas beforehand. Grasp the first few minutes to present the most critical information before the Dragons start asking too many questions.

The entrepreneurs must have a good understanding that by appearing/taping on *Dragons' Den*, they can be subjected to unforeseen criticism. They will not be in a position to withdraw their consent at any time.

It is also very important to accept the reality that their presentation will be edited at the discretion of the CBC. They have absolutely no control on the edited pitch to be aired both on the television and online.

For those who secure a deal on-stage, be aware of the subsequent process of due diligence, negotiation and finalization. I was aware of deals that fell apart after the on-screen handshake. The entrepreneurs are solely responsible for negotiating and closing the deal with the opt-in Dragon(s). Deals can also take several months to close and do not expect an immediate settlement.

Know your business idea inside and out. Stay focused and in control from start to end. Give your best shot and enjoy the experience. Leave with a winning smile regardless of the outcome.

Don'ts

Do not let the Dragon(s) take you too far from your presentation.

Most entrepreneurs may forget this important reminder. They can refuse an offer from a Dragon if they think the Dragon is not a suitable investor or the suggested deal is not right for them. Do not sell yourself short while at the same time do not over-estimate yourself.

No lawsuits or complaints should be filed against the CBC. It would be a waste of time and resources. Remember the entrepreneurs have signed a Consent & Release Form before taping.

Reminder

The Dragons are resistant and reluctant to part with their money. They will find every reason to reject a business proposal. Physical products do have an edge compared to a service or idea.

How Did We Do

For our first pitch, once we recovered from the initial shock, we stayed in control and were able to finish our presentation before tackling the Dragons' raised questions. I acted like a cool cucumber throughout the presentation even while some of the Dragons continued laughing. I was proud of Nelson's performance.

For our second pitch, Nelson out-performed and was competent in responding to the Dragons' questions. I was not happy with my performance because I let the Dragons divert the business proposal to my financial credentials.

Considering our business proposal was to partner with the Dragon(s) to promote a book on trading discipline and capital protection, the whole Q&A session was on investment terminologies at a wholesale level that are irrelevant to most retail investors.

I spent years in learning how to day trade Futures. I captured my ups and downs in this book especially the mistakes I made. This book was about not losing money. Its mission was to alert both inexperienced and experienced investors the importance of trading discipline, capital protection and money management.

As of this moment, I still have no clue why the Dragons did not see the merit of participating in a financial literacy movement that would help educate investors from different backgrounds.

Question: Will The Fiedler's be back to the Den ...

Sign-Up

SIGN-UP

I have included most of our props inclusive of the draft ones that were not used for our auditions and pitches. Readers will get an idea on the progress and very often the process involved lots of back-and-forth changes plus change of heart.

I apologize for the low-resolution black and white quality on the photos. Readers are welcome to visit my website bethfiedler.com and complete an access form.

You will enjoy free access to a *Taming The Dragons* portal with our pitch photos and rehearsal videos.

BIOGRAPHY ON NELSON

Nelson has been a dynamic and results-driven sales professional with an outstanding record of achievement and demonstrated success in highly competitive markets. He played an important customer service role when he was only five.

His father ran a deli business in the Kitchener/ Waterloo region when he was born. Nelson enjoyed interacting with people at an early age. Before completing his Bachelor's Degree in Electrical Engineering at the University of Waterloo, he already created a home portrait business serving thousands of happy customers.

His passion has always been in direct sales. His competence in a full sales cycle (from lead generation to post-sales customer support) and exceptional presentation skills have contributed to his amazing on-stage performances at the Den.

When you have access to our *Taming The Dragons* portal, you'll witness Nelson's quick wits and ability to adapt to a fast-paced production environment. Bear in mind that both pitches were one take performances. There were also last-minute change requests to our pitches minutes before we went on stage.

For our first pitch, Nelson did a magic trick in front of the five dragons. Kevin was invited to come down to our presentation area and he was only inches away from Nelson to detect any mishap. His magic performance went well and succeeded in turning a $20 note into a $100 note.

He was disappointed that his magic performance was not part of the pitch to be aired. However, I believe our readers would enjoy his trick when viewing our rehearsal videos (available after sign-up).

For our second chance pitch, Nelson was very prompt in incorporating Mike's habitual hand movement into his on-stage performance when we were facing the Dragons. We could tell Mike really liked Nelson as he threw him several questions.

Professional Accomplishments

Top Sales and Top Closing % Awards Winners on a consistent basis

Host of Futures trading webinars with attendees from different parts of the world

Academic Accomplishment

Bachelor of Applied Science
School of Electrical Engineering
University of Waterloo, Waterloo, Canada

nelsonfiedler.com

BIOGRAPHY ON BETH

Beth is a dynamic lady with extensive life experience in both Eastern and Western environments. She has lived and worked in three international cities (Beijing, Hong Kong and Toronto) and travelled extensively across 15+ countries (over 100 cities).

She has gained substantial insight into different organizational cultures and management practices from her various management positions and consultation projects. For example,

- General Manager
  Fleming International Limited
  Hong Kong and Shenzhen, PR China
- Assistant Vice President, Operations Management
  AIG Finance (Hong Kong) Limited, Hong Kong
- Senior Credit Administrator
  Swiss Bank Corporation (Canada), Toronto, Canada
- Employee Development
  Scotia Capital, Toronto, Canada
- Office Manager
  WJS International Inc, Beijing, PR China

Beth fell in love with training after years of Toastmasters learning. Her starting a consulting and soft skills training business (= leaving a senior management position with AIG) surprised a lot of people.

Beth has touched thousands of lives on a global basis. She inspired hundreds of people to become public speaking members. She was the owner and organizer of a multi-million HK$ Christmas function.

Her quality leadership and passion have attracted lots of media attention. Beth was interviewed by AlterMedic.com, *Hamilton Spectator* (a local newspaper in the Halton Region, Ontario, Canada), Metro Broadcast Hong Kong, Toronto CBCC, and *The Record* (a local newspaper of the Kitchener/Waterloo region in Ontario Canada). Stories about her vision were reported in *Hamilton Spectator, The Record, Oriental Daily, Apple Daily, Hong Kong Economic Times, The Sun, Sing Tao Daily, Ming Pao, Central Magazine, Eat & Travel, and Sisters*. Her most recent media appearances were on the CBC *Dragons' Den* (Toronto), Seasons VIII and IX.

Beth is known for her big heart in sharing. She has a strong passion for helping others excel!

Professional Accomplishments

Area Governor of the Year, Toastmasters International, Pan-Southeast Asia Pacific Region

Distinguished Toastmaster (DTM), Toastmasters International, Hong Kong Division

Distinguished President's Area Award, Toastmasters International USA

Co-chair of the First District Toastmasters Convention in Hong Kong, Toastmasters International, Pan-Southeast Asia Pacific Region

Champion of an Inter-club Evaluation Contest, Toastmasters International, Hong Kong

Designer/Facilitator of over 150 Experiential Training Programs, Facilitation Sessions and Speaking Assignments (Canada, China PRC, Macau, Pan-Southeast Asia Pacific Region, Saudi Arabia, Taiwan ROC, The Philippines and USA)

Organizer/Advisor of over 200 Public and Private Functions (up to 7,000 participants) (Canada, China PRC, Macau, Pan-Southeast Asia Pacific Region, Taiwan ROC, Thailand, The Philippines and USA)

Academic Accomplishments

Bachelor of Applied Arts (Hons)
School of Administration and Information Management
Ryerson University, Toronto, Canada

Diploma in Adult Training and Development
University of Toronto, Toronto, Canada

Certified Social Media Strategist
Social Media Marketing University, USA

Certificates in Teaching English to Speakers of Other
Languages (TESOL)
TESL, Ottawa, Canada
Trinity College London, England

Canadian Securities Course (Hons)
The Canadian Securities Institute, Toronto, Canada

Diploma in Multimedia Web Site Design
Unisoft Education Center, Hong Kong

bethfiedler.com
wp-winpro.weebly.com

www.ingramcontent.com/pod-product-compliance
Lightning Source LLC
Chambersburg PA
CBHW070933210326
41520CB00021B/6926